Gun

Mastery Learning in the Science Classroom

Success for Every Student

Mastery Learning in the Science Classroom

Success for Every Student

Kelly Morgan

NSTApress
National Science Teachers Association

Arlington, Virginia

National Science Teachers Association

Claire Reinburg, Director
Jennifer Horak, Managing Editor
Andrew Cooke, Senior Editor
Judy Cusick, Senior Editor
Wendy Rubin, Associate Editor
Amy America, Book Acquisitions Coordinator

ART AND DESIGN
Will Thomas Jr., Director
Joe Butera, Senior Graphic Designer, cover and interior design
Cover illustration by Leon Tura for iStock.

PRINTING AND PRODUCTION
Catherine Lorrain, Director

NATIONAL SCIENCE TEACHERS ASSOCIATION
Francis Q. Eberle, PhD, Executive Director
David Beacom, Publisher

Library of Congress Cataloging-in-Publication Data
Morgan, Kelly, 1977-
  Mastery learning in the science classroom: success for every student/ by Kelly Morgan.
    p. cm.
  Includes bibliographical references.
  ISBN 978-1-936137-09-1
  1. Science—Study and teaching. 2. Mastery learning. I. Title.
  Q181 . M78 2011
  507.1—dc22

                    2010044007

eISBN 978-1-936137-53-4

NSTA is committed to publishing material that promotes the best in inquiry-based science education. However, conditions of actual use may vary, and the safety procedures and practices described in this book are intended to serve only as a guide. Additional precautionary measures may be required. NSTA and the authors do not warrant or represent that the procedures and practices in this book meet any safety code or standard of federal, state, or local regulations. NSTA and the authors disclaim any liability for personal injury or damage to property arising out of or relating to the use of this book, including any of the recommendations, instructions, or materials contained therein.

PERMISSIONS

Contents

Contents

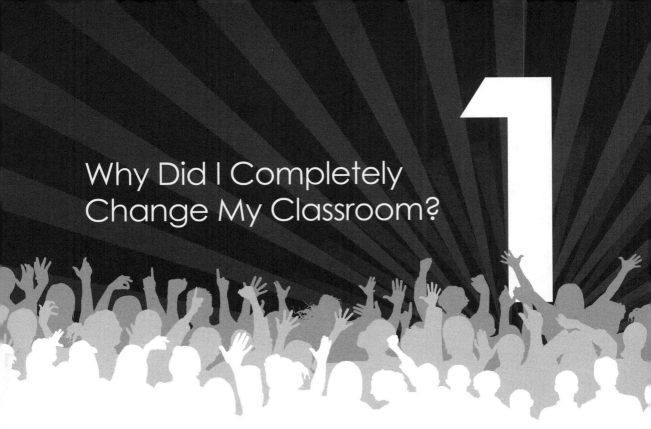

Why Did I Completely Change My Classroom?

I'd like to start out by saying a few things about my experience with mastery learning. First, mastery learning is not new; it's been around for a very long time and many teachers may be using various aspects of it, consciously or not. I didn't invent it, and I've learned a lot about how to use it from other people.

Second, my teaching experience is with high school physical science and chemistry courses, but teachers at all grade levels and in all subjects can use mastery learning. There are some particular aspects of teaching science (like those labs!) that more general books on mastery learning may not touch on, and that's why I wrote this book.

Because my experience is limited to high school physical sciences, I have developed a website to facilitate sharing and communication concerning mastery teaching in the sciences. This website gives teachers of various levels and disciplines the opportunity to share, ask questions, and support one another as they venture into the world of mastery learning. You can join this community at *www.ScienceMasteryLearning.com*.

The Questions That Led to Change

By many accounts, I was a successful teacher during my first eight years. I am nationally board-certified and have a master's degree and a PhD. My students liked me and my class. I taught in a thematic manner to tightly integrate real-world applications with college-prep chemistry content. I frequently used inquiry and student-designed experiments in my classes. Most of my students learned, as evidenced by assessments throughout and at the end of the courses. I used effective techniques such as visual PowerPoint presentations with extensive examples, guided practice, and scaffolding for inquiry.

So why did I decide to completely turn my classroom upside down during year 9? Because *most* of my students were learning—but not all. And because I didn't like the answers to some of the questions I was asking myself.

Were my students learning or passing?

My class had been set up in a fairly typical manner—class discussions and lectures, lab about once a week, in-class guided practice, students working together in small groups to practice, chapter reviews, and traditional exams. My grading usually consisted of about 20% for practice, 30% for labs, 40% for tests, and 10% for the final exam.

The problem with this scenario is that students could copy all the practice and review problems from a friend and ride on the coattails of a lab partner for lab grades, and if they received 100% on all practice and labs they only needed to average 20% on the tests and final exam to pass the class. Even if they got 90% on practice and labs, they only had to score 30% on the chapter tests to pass the course.

Students could copy all their nontest work from friends and dramatically fail every test and still walk out of my classroom with chemistry credit. I was "putting my stamp of approval" on these students. I could solve the problem by stopping copying on practice and labs (but let's face it—those who want to will always find a way to cheat the system in some way) or by weighting the grade so heavily toward tests that those who did not do well would not pass the class. I did not like the second option because weighting the test more heavily would unfairly lower the grade of students who truly did all the course work themselves yet didn't test well. For similar reasons, I have always believed in partial credit on the tests themselves—which usually allowed most students to receive at least the 20–30% needed to pass the class with such a system.

Was I building the needed prior knowledge for my students?

During my PhD course work, I read a lot of interesting research and information. Most of it contained elements that I had already known through years in the classroom, but the readings would put several pieces together or give some new light to an old observation, and I learned a great deal. I read about the importance of prior knowledge. I knew that what students already know is a huge factor in how well they do on new information—but studying cognition and how we learn brought this key factor into greater focus.

So much of what I do in my chemistry and physical science courses depends on the previous chapters. If students never really "get" how to write a chemical formula, how can I go on to chemical reactions, balancing, stoichiometry, and other topics requiring that basic skill? The kids who were left behind in the beginning *never* caught up. So why was I leaving them behind? Because once a majority of the kids "get it" in a "traditional classroom," you need to keep going. You tend to teach to the middle in a heterogeneous classroom, and once the middle is ready, you move on to the next topic.

What messages was I sending to my students?

I was sending many nonverbal messages to my students that were unconscious on my part: It's OK to go through this class without ever really learning. Everyone learns the same way and requires the same activities. We're going to move on even if some of you are not ready. I'm not going to let those who are ready faster move on before the middle is ready. I don't expect you all to be able to understand all of this information, so I don't hold you to higher standards than copying daily work and labs along with failing every test.

These were not the messages I wanted to send! Instead, now I stand in front of my students on the first day of class and tell them that I believe that every student in my room can learn the chemistry in this course. That even if they never take another chemistry class, I want them to walk out of the room believing that they were capable of learning this material and that they *did* learn it. I explicitly tell them that every student will get at least an 80% on every quiz in the class and that I'm not going to move on without them—I'll keep working with them until they do get it. This is a very powerful message to send to students who have barely passed their previous science courses, believe they aren't good at it, and are scared to death just to be in a chemistry class.

I also tell the higher-level students that they can move on when they're ready. They don't have to wait for everyone else. If they don't need to practice balancing equations for two days before they can pass a quiz, then they don't need to do so. This is an equally powerful message to send to these students, who often feel held back in many of their courses. Yes, there are often honors courses advanced students can take—but within every level of course, there are various levels of students. Even in an honors course some are ready to move on before others.

I let all the students know that I understand that students learn in different ways and at different speeds. And that what one person gets easily or struggles with may vary from section to section or chapter to chapter.

There is a huge learning curve at the beginning for students, because they are not used to this format of class and don't know how to operate within it right away. But they get it after a while—and when they do, they are grateful for this class structure.

Why Did I Completely Change My Classroom?

Who was taking responsibility for their learning?

For years I held all the responsibility for my students' learning: I decided when they needed more practice, I decided how they were to learn a concept, and I decided when they were ready to move on. If I was going to help prepare these students for "life outside of high school"—whatever that may look like for each student—I was going to have to help them begin to take responsibility for their own learning.

That doesn't mean that they are on their own. I guide them—for example, suggesting that they work on a worksheet to check their ability to calculate density before taking the density quiz; or pointing out how a narrated PowerPoint presentation, which allows electrons to move around on the screen, might be a good way to learn how to draw dot structures for molecules. If they don't pass their first quiz, I suggest that they do some more learning, thinking, or discussing before coming back for another quiz. By the end of the year, students are much more capable of determining whether they know the material and are ready for a quiz or need more practice, help, or discussion before taking the quiz. I believe that these self-monitoring skills will serve them well as they prepare for their next stage in life.

Am I sure I want to do this?

Even with all of these reasons to make the transition to a mastery learning classroom, it was not easy. I wavered back and forth many, many times that July and August before I implemented this type of classroom. It was scary—how was I going to handle grading, quizzing, instruction, and (for goodness' sake) those labs?! Would my students learn as much, less, more? I worried about "hurting" my students academically, despite the fact that all the research I'd studied and all my own personal classroom experiences were suggesting that it would be a good thing.

I've presented much of this information at various conferences and workshops and I see the same look in many teachers' eyes that I must have had in my own—I really feel like this will change things for the better…but am I sure I really want to jump off this cliff? What about…? What about…? There are a lot of things to think about, and I hope that this book will go a long way toward answering the questions I had and the questions other teachers have asked me. I'll share research-based teaching techniques and the things I've learned about how to run a mastery-based classroom on a day-to-day basis.

Using This Book

Chapter 2 gives an overview of mastery learning, its history and effects on students. It's a brief introduction to the general teaching method and should be read first.

Chapter 3 delves into a great deal of research that supports the various components of mastery learning. You may or may not wish to skip this chapter at first. I love research and always want to know the basis behind teaching techniques before I delve into the nitty-gritty details, so I would read it before moving on to the more practical chapters. However, I realize that many readers will be anxious to see exactly how a mastery class would play out in real life and may be bored, frankly, with the review of research supporting the methods. If you're that type of person, go ahead and skip Chapter 3 and come back to it when you're curious about why various aspects of mastery learning work.

Chapter 4 is a "frequently asked questions" type of chapter. When I've presented on mastery learning in the science classroom and informally talked with colleagues, there are many details about the day-to-day workings of a mastery classroom that are often asked. This chapter takes you through as many as I could think of to help you get started.

Chapter 5 pulls it all together to give you a picture of what a mastery learning science classroom might look like. Read this chapter to see what a typical day in a mastery classroom might feel like. There are also several variations presented for implementation of mastery learning at different levels. I hope these snapshots into my vision of how mastery learning operates will spark your imagination and creativity for how you might make these teaching methods your own.

Mastery Learning

2

What Is Mastery Learning?

The key to mastery learning is that students are required to show mastery of a concept before they are allowed to move on to the next concept. The teacher determines at what level the mastery must be accomplished—for example, 100%, 80%, or 70%. Students are given opportunities to learn the material through a variety of instructional strategies and then take the quiz. If students do not show mastery of the concept, then they are given additional instruction or resources and allowed to take the quiz (usually in another form) again. Mastery learning can be either teacher-paced or student-paced, or a blend of the two. The various forms of a mastery class will be discussed in greater depth in Chapters 4 and 5 of this book.

Self-Paced Is Not Self-Taught

Mastery learning is not a self-taught class. I have more interactions with individual students and small groups of students in an instructional capacity than in a conventional classroom. Although students have access to resources such as narrated PowerPoint presentations, reading guides for their text, and practice worksheets, this system does not mean that they are learning on their own. They know that at any point they may ask a question, ask for an explanation of something, request that I work out an example, or discuss information with their peers. It is not that they do not need a teacher and can learn it on their own—it is that *they each need a teacher in a different way and at different points in time.* Their needs for teacher interaction vary with the content they are studying and their comfort with the underlying concepts or math skills necessary.

History of Mastery Learning

As with most things in education, mastery learning is not new. There were various systems for mastery learning in the 1920s and 1930s; one example is the Winnetka Plan developed by Carleton Washburne (Block 1971). Two prominent systems emerged in the 1960s: Bloom's Learning for Mastery (LFM; Bloom 1968) and Keller's Personalized System of Instruction (PSI; Keller 1968). Bloom's LFM was mostly a teacher-paced system with the teacher presenting the information. Students who did not show mastery had additional individual or group tutoring before attempting the quiz again. Keller's PSI mainly used written material. Students who did not show mastery worked through the same material before attempting the quiz again.

According to Bloom (1968), a conventional course contains a normal distribution of aptitude, yet the instruction is the same for each student. The outcome of a conventional course is a normal distribution of performance that correlates with that of aptitude. A mastery course, Bloom stated, would have the same normal distribution of aptitude but, because instruction was tailored for each student, the final performance would be universally high for all students. Lower-aptitude students would require more time in the beginning of the course as they gained the foundational concepts and (most likely) made up for lower prior knowledge. However, as these lower-aptitude students progressed through the course, having mastered the fundamental concepts, the extra time needed for these students would lessen or even disappear.

Effects of Mastery Learning

Most of the research on mastery learning systems occurred in the 1970s and 1980s. One group completed a meta-analysis of 108 different experimental studies of mastery learning compared with the conventional classroom (Kulik, Kulik, and Bangert-Drowns 1990). Of the 103 studies that used final exam performance in their study, there was an average effect size of 0.52. Effect size (the difference in averages between two groups divided by the average standard deviations of the two groups) is a measure of how many standard deviations the group has moved.

An effect size of 0.52 is considered a moderate effect (0.2 is minimal, 0.5 is moderate, and 0.8 is large). Another way to think of this 0.52 effect size of mastery learning is to think about the average student. In the mastery learning class, the average student performed at the 70th percentile; in the conventional class the average student was defined as the 50th percentile (Kulik, Kulik, and Bangert-Drowns 1990). The mastery learning classes had their *average* student performing at an *equivalent level of the top 30%* of the conventional class—that's quite a jump! When the researchers disaggregated their data by student ability level, they found that lower-level students often made the biggest improvements.

In the meta-analysis, there were 11 studies in which follow-up exams were administered about eight weeks after the instruction ended (Kulik, Kulik, and

Bangert-Drowns 1990). For these studies, the mastery class showed an effect size of 0.60 at the end of the course and an effect size of 0.71 on the follow-up exam. Mastery students still outperformed students from a traditional course, with an increasingly greater gap, eight weeks after the course was over.

Mastery Learning's Pendulum Swings

With such amazing data showing that students in a mastery class perform better, even after eight weeks without instruction, why is mastery learning not prevalent now? Like any educational trend, the pendulum swings from one side to another. Amid the great results in the early years, curriculum publishers began to produce "PSI materials" in the ancillary packages that accompanied their texts (Gallup and Allan 1996). Needless to say, not all of these materials were well designed, and teachers not trained in the methodologies of mastery learning became frustrated. Teachers complained of low-level assessment that accompanied the publisher-created PSI resources, despite the fact that most publisher-created assessments are low-level—this was not unique to the PSI resources they created. Untrained teachers using poor resources is a prescription for frustration and leads to teachers and schools discontinuing the method.

Another reason for mastery learning's loss of favor is that it takes a teacher, even one familiar with the technique, a great deal of time to prepare for a mastery class the first time it is to be offered. Although this burden is much lighter in subsequent course offerings, it does take much more effort that first year. This increased effort can be a barrier to using mastery learning.

A third reason for mastery learning's loss of favor is a little surprising: It worked *too* well in many cases. More students passed courses and knew more as a result of the mastery learning structure than those passing the same courses in the past. The students coming out of mastery learning courses then moved on to upper-level courses with different skill sets than the upper-level courses were designed for. Also, students enrolled in mastery learning courses at the expense of enrollment numbers in other courses. Instructors using mastery methods were often met with hostility from more traditional classroom instructors due to the different results and student attitudes. Howard Gallup, PhD, a psychology professor at Lafayette College, gave an example at an address to the psychology club:

> Henry Pennypacker managed to get the entire set of general education courses taken during the first two years at the University of Florida in PSI format. Florida's admissions policy was that anyone who had finished high school could enroll at the university. By the end of the first year, the typical dropout rate was up around 80%. Under PSI, that dropped to about 15%. This meant that the university now had many thousands of students wanting to continue with upper level courses. PSI was discontinued after two years. (Gallup 1995)

Current Research

Due to mastery learning "falling out of favor," there has not been a research focus on this teaching method. However, many of the aspects of mastery learning that were found to provide the highest effect sizes in previous studies (Kulik, Kulik, and Bangert-Drowns 1990) are continuing to be researched. These include performance-based feedback, efficient learning principles, scaffolding, and differentiation of content based on prior knowledge. The research on any one of these aspects is providing important information for teaching—and combining all of them into mastery learning would not negate their positive effects. These specific components of mastery learning will be discussed in the next chapter.

It is important to note that mastery learning, and research on it, was not stopped because it didn't work. In fact, it is quite the opposite. The meta-analysis of 108 independent studies of the effects of mastery learning showed that it has moderate to large positive effects on student performance (Kulik, Kulik, and Bangert-Drowns 1990). It is not that new studies showed information to the contrary, but rather the bandwagon/pendulum phenomenon discussed above and the amount of effort necessary to initially implement this type of course have pushed mastery learning to the background.

Connection With National Science Education Standards and Standards-Based Education

Since the mid-1990s, there has been a significant movement toward standards-based education. The National Science Education Standards (NSES) (National Research Council 1996) and state science standards, most often developed to align with the NSES, resulted in district and course standards. State assessments and the No Child Left Behind Act of 2001 have given a greater emphasis to education for every student to meet minimum content standards.

Mastery learning is a wonderful complement to standards-based education. Mastery learning is based on the concept of holding every student to a standard of performance rather than simply exposing every student to the minimum required content. If students are held to mastery standards throughout a course that align with the standards on which they will be assessed, this will ensure that the course is meeting standards-based education requirements. However, the benefit of mastery learning as opposed to simply "teaching to the test" is that higher-level students are not held back as all students are moved through required content. Students who can demonstrate mastery of the baseline requirements can then move on to more advanced topics in a course, while students who require more time to meet those minimum competencies are allowed that time and support.

NSES Revision Process

As of the writing of this book, it's been 14 years since the NSES were released. The changes in access and availability of information, understanding of effective and efficient learning, and technology in those 14 years are simply astounding. The National Research Council (NRC) has appointed an 18-member panel, supported by teams in the various science disciplines, to write the framework for the next set of national science standards. The framework is to be completed in early 2011, and the writing of the actual standards will begin at that time.

The revised science standards will focus on core ideas and themes that weave through the science disciplines. The core ideas will then be broken down into specific progressions across grade levels. The aim for the new standards is depth rather than breadth, as well as cohesive understanding of the core ideas.

The development of the new framework and standards will undoubtedly affect science teachers and courses everywhere. The National Science Teachers Association (NSTA) will continue to post information concerning the process (and from time to time facilitate gathering feedback from various stakeholders, such as teachers and administrators) on their website (*www.nsta.org*). You do not need to be an NSTA member to access this information.

Teaching Broader Skills for the Future

I aim to teach more than just science in my classroom. I realize that not very many of my chemistry students will go on to become chemists some day, but there are many skills that I can help them acquire. In "naming" these skills I hesitate to use educational terminology, because we teachers all know how an idea can be given a catchy name and become a "fad" even though no one is really sure what it means; it may be pushed on teachers without precise and concise definitions and with little or no concrete support, and after its time in the sun it fades away (which, by the way, is what happened to this not-new idea of mastery learning, as you may recall from earlier in this chapter!). But the skills I'm talking about helping my students acquire have been in the educational pool of "hot terms" lately and are known as *21st century skills*. You may have heard the term and been a little unclear as to what it really means, and you may have asked people what it means and been given a rather hand-waving vague explanation; or you may have a clear understanding of it all (in which case, please share with all those teachers around you!).

I looked up *21st century skills* at the Partnership for 21st Century Skills website (*www.p21.org/index.php*) to gain a better understanding of what people mean by this term. Among the curricular, interdisciplinary, critical-thinking, and application (such as engineering and technology) skills the organization promotes, I found the following "life and career skills" that fit my own vague, hand-waving explanation of these "other skills" I've been trying to help my students acquire:

- Flexibility and Adaptability. Flexibility and adaptability are a cornerstone of my interpretation of mastery learning. I don't use the overly prescribed versions of mastery learning that were shot down by frustrated teachers in the past (students read passage A, take the quiz, fail the quiz, and return to passage A again to learn from it this time). My version of mastery learning includes options for how to learn in various ways that are flexible and adaptable to the students' background knowledge, abilities, and preferences.

- Initiative and Self-Direction. Mastery learning requires the students to take the initiative—for example, they choose which activities they're going to complete, and they determine when they are ready to take the quiz and attempt to move on. Students are self-directed as they choose which learning opportunities to experience.

- Social and Cross-Cultural Skills. Rather than assigning lab partners or letting students choose their own partners, I structured my mastery learning classroom as a fluid set of small groups. Students who passed moved out of a group, while others in the group who did not pass sought out another group working on the same content. They learned social skills of working with whomever was at the same point of learning—not waiting until their friend caught up or assuming they were ready to move on just because their group did. This dynamic, and often self-directed, grouping process gave students an abundance of practice at social skills. Also, don't forget the key social skills of politeness and patience, which they had to practice as they waited for my attention if I was grading another student's test or working with another group!

- Productivity and Accountability. Students are held completely accountable for their own learning in mastery learning. I did not move on when the majority of students were ready, as in a traditional class. My students could not float through the class, as some had done in the past. They were accountable and had to be productive in order to progress through the course.

- Leadership and Responsibility. Students were responsible for their own learning. There was no way they could not be. They chose which activities to do to learn the content. They determined when they were ready for a quiz, not me. They requested the quizzes. They requested the labs when they were ready. My students were responsible for tracking their own progress and for keeping an appropriate pace in the course (with a little prodding from time to time if they started to slip, of course).

By the end of the school year I saw dramatic improvements in these 21st century skills, compared with previous years teaching in a traditional format. These results alone were enough to convince me that this is the best way for me to run my classroom. The next two chapters will take you through research underlying the "nuts and bolts" of mastery learning and how I achieved those results.

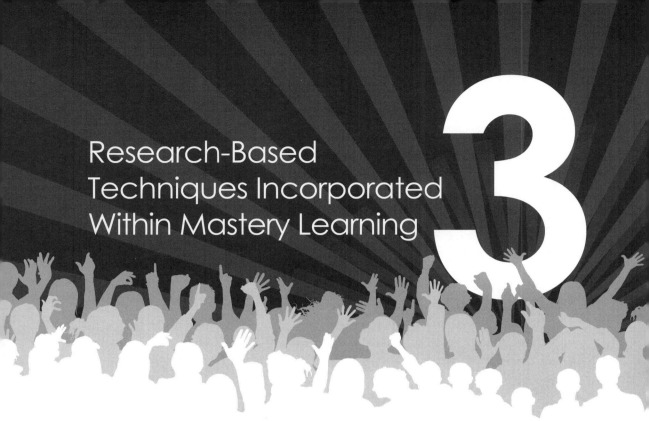

Research-Based Techniques Incorporated Within Mastery Learning

3

This chapter begins with a brief explanation of cognition and how we learn. This explanation will serve as the foundation for understanding why the various aspects of mastery learning have the impact that they do. For a much more complete understanding of attention, motivation, learning, and other aspects of cognition and best teaching practices, teachers should refer to *The Unified Learning Model* (Shell et al. 2010).

Cognition: How We Process and Learn Information

Bruning et al. describe cognitive processing in their textbook *Cognitive Psychology and Instruction* (2004). Incoming information is initially processed in sensory memory. Once the sensory system perceives the stimulus, it is processed within working memory. Working memory activates information stored in long-term memory that is associated with the current information-processing task. Our ability to process information, therefore, is constrained by the capacity of working memory. However, as information is grouped together through "chunking," or processes become automatic through large amounts of practice, less working memory is required. As a result, people are able to overcome the limited capacity of working memory for the pieces of information we can process at any given time.

Types of Cognitive Load

There are three types of load placed on working memory: intrinsic, extraneous, and germane (Van Merrienboar, Kester, and Paas 2006). *Intrinsic load* refers to task difficulty. A multistep task has a much higher intrinsic load than a single-step task. However, the level of chunking in the person's long-term memory can reduce the intrinsic load of even a large, multistep problem (see next section for more on how chunking works). In this way, intrinsic load is dependent on the person undertaking the task as well as the nature of the task.

Extraneous load is not necessary for the task to be completed—the elements causing extraneous load can be removed and the task is still possible. Extraneous load can be due to a variety of factors, such as unclear directions, poor instructional design, distractions present during the task, and personal emotions and thoughts.

Germane load refers to the load placed on working memory to learn (create or alter schemas) and to encode information in a meaningful manner. Germane load is the load of "learning." If you've ever helped students through a problem or exercise and at the end they honestly have no idea what they just did, there is a good chance they had no room for germane load in their working memory and therefore didn't "learn" anything. If the intrinsic and extraneous loads are too high, there will be no room for the cognitive load of connecting new information with a previous schema—altering that schema, forming new schemas, or connecting various schema together.

Chunking of information

The processing of information occurs in the working memory. The more exposure or practice a person has with a concept or task, the greater the likelihood that some of the information or process becomes "chunked." When information is chunked, various parts of the concept or task are linked together in memory and accessing or processing one part will access the remainder.

You can see chunking vividly when watching a toddler learn how to walk. Any distraction—a dog barking, a person cheering for them, or sometimes even just a blink—will cause the toddler to fall down. At that moment, it takes all of the toddler's working memory to keep his or her balance and control the body to walk. Any other input that the toddler attends to will push out the information necessary to remain balanced. However, after practice, the toddler will be able to walk, talk, and chew gum at the same time (as the saying goes). The processes of walking have been chunked together—and through an enormous amount of practice have become automatic. This means that the one task of walking no longer overwhelms the toddler's working memory. It doesn't mean that the task of walking is any different—the task itself hasn't changed—but because the information has been chunked and practiced until it became automatic, it doesn't take up as much working memory space.

Processing information in working memory and prior knowledge

When information is attended to in working memory, it activates relevant information in long-term memory to be used in working memory to process the new information or stimuli. If the information in long-term memory is relatively unfamiliar to the person, it will take up a larger amount of space (number of "slots") in working memory. For example, when a student who is just learning order of operations is given an expression to simplify, he or she must remember the order of operations and how to apply them to that specific expression. However, when the teacher is given the same expression to simplify, he or she processes the same information (order of operations and how to apply them) much more quickly—perhaps even automatically. The student may not be able to attend to any other information while completing the task, whereas the teacher may be able to keep an eye on the clock, listen to the students whispering in the back of the room, and think about where he or she will go next in the lesson. It's not that people who can do the task, such as simplifying an expression, have a much greater working memory capacity; it is that they have the information chunked together and therefore that same information takes less space within the working memory.

Although intrinsic load refers to the difficulty of the task itself, the expertise and knowledge of the person undertaking the task and the person's ability to chunk the information will affect the intrinsic load placed on that person's working memory. Think of the teacher and the student simplifying the expression. Not only does the teacher *not* have a dramatically different working memory capacity that makes the task "easier" for the teacher, but the task itself is also no different—it's the same expression they're both being asked to solve. What causes the difference is the prior knowledge (in a chunked form) the teacher holds; for example, the teacher may have simplified similar expressions before and have something to which he or she can compare the new expression. This chunking of information and prior experiences is what we refer to when we talk about prior knowledge.

Consider the cognitive load placed on an experienced teacher versus a student when designing an investigation. A teacher experienced at designing laboratory investigations for her students has chunks of information concerning the science content, the process of investigation design, the availability of tools and equipment, common laboratory techniques that are applicable, prior experiences with similar laboratory investigations, an awareness of what background knowledge the students will or will not have, where students are likely to misunderstand instructions or make a mistake, and so on. Perhaps the teacher's process of designing an investigation for students has become automatic through years of practice. These chunks of information and automaticity of processing allow the teacher to process information concerning the results section, what will be needed in the data table, and the steps needed to gather the data while she is creating the materials list near the beginning of the investigation.

Consider the same scientific investigation design from the point of view of a student. He does not have the automaticity of design process. He likely does not have information concerning the science concepts, lab techniques, or common requirements of an investigation. Thus, the design of the same scientific investigation will put a much greater demand on his working memory than on the teacher's.

Prior knowledge does affect the intrinsic difficulty of a problem. There are two ways to lower the intrinsic load (difficulty) of a problem: (1) decrease the difficulty of the problem, often by breaking the problem down or providing scaffolding (discussed later in this chapter); or (2) increase the prior knowledge of the person.

The Importance of Understanding a Student's Prior Knowledge

Now that we understand how working memory capacity limits our processing ability, we can see how vitally important prior knowledge is for a student. Often, we have very heterogeneous populations in our schools. I taught in a school that had rural, urban, and suburban students within its boundaries. Imagine that you are teaching in such a district and you're teaching a unit on weather. You have two students in front of you—one of them grew up in a farming family and the other in a suburban setting. For the student from the farming family, weather is a daily factor in the family's livelihood—it affects every aspect of their work on the farm (e.g., whether they can harvest this week or have to wait another week). This student has heard people discussing weather changes, watches the weather reports each day with his family while watching the news, and has learned what weather will come after he hears someone say "a low pressure system is moving in."

The student from the suburban setting has a different relationship with weather. Perhaps her parents don't get home from work until after the evening news is over and the student chooses to watch shows other than the news in their absence. The weather does not affect the family's livelihood or, for the most part, their daily tasks. Beyond knowing that she needs a coat because it's chilly outside, the weather does not play an important role in this student's life.

When you begin to talk about weather in your classroom, the first student will immediately have images and information that are called into working memory from long-term memory when processing your new information. The second student, however, has nothing to "hang" the new information on—no existing schema to connect it with. For the first student, it may be a simple matter of applying correct vocabulary to phenomena and concepts that he is already familiar with from his daily life. For the second student, it all is new and abstract. The first student will be able to process more information at one time in working memory with chunking and relevant schemas already in place. The second student will require much smaller chunks of new information, and her lack of relevant schemas will need to be taken into account when the teacher explains concepts.

All teachers know that it is impossible to meet every student's needs while teaching the whole class. We cannot keep the students with greater background knowledge interested and engaged when they are "bored" with stuff they already know and understand. We usually "teach to the middle"—but doing so ignores the lack of background knowledge in some students and, as a result, they cannot learn the new knowledge we're presenting, which means they won't catch up. We all know it, many complain about it; but most of us feel powerless to do anything about it. A teacher is only one person, and there are so many students and so much content to get through.

Mastery learning takes care of these problems. It's not that it doesn't raise other significant logistical issues (which will be discussed in the next chapter), but it does solve the problem of having to hold back the student with greater prior knowledge while spending more time with students who have lower levels of relevant schemas to build their knowledge base. Each student is where he or she is, and the teacher works with where the students are to get them to where they need to be. It's not about "what can you learn in a given time period" but rather "what do you need to learn this." It changes the lens through which you view your students—it's not a race, but a matter of what resources, background information or experiences, and support a student needs to get to where you want him or her to be.

As Bloom's research showed (Bloom 1968), once the teacher takes the time to help the lower-level students catch up with the foundational knowledge, these students don't require extra time for subsequent concepts. They do not always take longer to learn material. I have seen it my classroom—in the beginning they are much more spread out in level of background knowledge, but as students gain foundational knowledge (and just as importantly, confidence when they are not left behind), they catch up to—and sometimes pass—other students.

Efficient Learning and Mastery Learning

With our understanding of the limited capabilities of working memory to process great amounts of information simultaneously while still saving room for learning, we now look at some ways to maximize the effects of a student's efforts within a mastery classroom. This is but a very brief introduction to efficient learning, and teachers are urged to read more information on the principles of efficient learning in the book *Efficiency in Learning: Evidence-Based Guidelines to Manage Cognitive Load* (Clark, Nguyen, and Sweller 2006).

Breaking concepts down and scaffolding

In 1930 Vygotsky (1978, p. 86) described the *zone of proximal development* as "the distance between the actual developmental level as determined by independent problem solving and the level of potential development as determined through problem solving under adult guidance or in collaboration with more capable peers. The zone represents the potential for a child's development when aided by others."

Scaffolding is "the precise help that enables a learner to achieve a specific goal that would not be possible without some kind of support" (Sharpe 2006, p. 212). Although Wood, Bruner, and Ross (1976) did not use the term *zone of proximal development* in their presentation of scaffolding, many authors have since made this connection (e.g., Sharpe 2006). Scaffolding can be seen as the assistance that is needed for the learner to succeed in the zone of proximal development. For scaffolding to be effective, it must place the learner within his or her zone of proximal development. Too much support results in the task becoming less challenging; not giving enough support results in anxiety and frustration for the learner (McNeill et al. 2006). One of the key characteristics of effective scaffolding is the removal of it. The goal of scaffolding is to, over time, push students' abilities (and zone of proximal development) further so that they no longer require the same level of scaffolding as they did before.

A mastery learning classroom provides a wonderful setting for scaffolding based on individual learners. In a classroom where "same" is no longer synonymous with "fair," it is possible to scaffold individual students. Some students may need more time, support, resources, and practice than others to master a concept. An individualized system, such as a mastery classroom can be, provides opportunities for such differentiated learning.

How and when to practice

It is common belief that practice makes perfect and that students need lots of practice to master skills. However, it is not so commonly understood how instructionally expensive practice is and which methods of practice are most efficient. Practice problems place demand on working memory that may be counterproductive to learning in a couple of ways (Clark, Nguyen, and Sweller 2006).

First, requiring practice of someone with low prior knowledge imposes a large intrinsic load and therefore does not "save room for learning" by allowing germane load. This is seen when students are guided through or perform the steps to solve a problem but then have no idea what they did or why. They didn't learn anything from the experience of solving the problem because the act of solving the problem itself was filling their working memory.

Students with low levels of prior knowledge learn much more efficiently by studying worked examples. However, it's difficult to get students to study worked examples in a meaningful way. One way to do this is to teach self-question techniques that allow the student to interact with the worked example, such as asking "Where did that number come from?" or "Why did they do that step next?" The actual working out of the problem and the determination of which steps to follow has been completed for them, and they are then free to use their working memory to learn from the solution rather than simply stumble through it.

Another way to encourage student interaction with worked examples is to use backwards-faded worked examples. In these types of worked examples, students are provided with completely worked-out examples, and then in subsequent examples steps are removed starting with the final step of the problem. An example of this type of worksheet is included in the appendix. Removing one step at a time creates a need for the student to self-question the completely worked-out examples to determine how to complete the partially worked-out examples. When the problems become more difficult (such as in the example worksheet when the problems required two steps), more support is given to the student to compensate for the increased mental load of the more difficult problem. This method of gradually increasing the intrinsic demand of the problem as the knowledge base of the student increases by using worked examples is supported by research findings to be a more efficient and effective way of learning problem solving than being given full problems to work out (Renkl, Atkinson, and Maier 2000).

The second way practice problems can be counterproductive to learning is a result of the *expertise reversal effect* (Kalyuga et al. 2003), in which providing instruction such as worked examples to someone who is already competent at that skill actually increases the demand on the working memory system and depresses performance. We cannot, therefore, provide the same practice material to all students and be sure that all students will benefit from it. In fact, it's likely that we can be sure that *not* all students will benefit.

Mastery learning classrooms, as described in the next two chapters, can provide the opportunity to individualize the amount and type of practice (as well as other forms of instruction) to provide efficient instruction to students of all levels.

The Dramatic Effect of Feedback and Individualized Instruction on Student Performance

A study was completed in 1984 to look at what's called the *2 sigma problem* (Bloom 1984). The study looked at a conventional classroom, a formative assessment–feedback classroom, and individual tutorial instruction. The conventional class-room was one instructor with approximately 30 students with periodic summative test-ing. The formative assessment–feedback classroom used the same instruction format as the conventional classroom (often with the same teachers) but with formative testing followed by corrective feedback and then follow-up testing. The tutorial instruction consisted of one tutor with one to three students and used the same formative testing–feedback-testing cycle as the formative assessment–feedback class in the study.

The study found that stu-dents in the formative assess-ment–feedback classroom per-formed one sigma (one standard deviation) better than the conven-tional classroom. The students in the tutorial instruction performed two sigma (two standard devia-tions) better than those in the con-ventional classroom. What this means is that 90% of the students in the tutorial instruction group and 70% of the students in the formative assessment–feedback classroom performed as well as the *highest* 20% of students in the conventional classroom. By using

TABLE 3.1	
Effect of Selected Alterable Variables on Student Achievement	
Variable	**Effect size**
Tutorial instruction	2.00
Reinforcement	1.20
Formative assessment—feedback classroom	1.00
Cues and explanations	1.00
Student classroom participation	1.00
Student time on task	1.00
Improved reading/study skills	1.00
Cooperative learning	0.80
Homework (graded)	0.80
Classroom morale	0.60
Initial cognitive prerequisites	0.60
Home environment intervention	0.50
Peer and cross-age remedial tutoring	0.40
Homework (assigned)	0.30
Higher-order questions	0.30
New science and math curricula	0.30
Teacher expectancy	0.30
Peer-group influence	0.20
Advance organizers	0.20
Socioeconomic status (for contrast)	0.25
Source: Adapted from Bloom 1984.	

formative assessment with meaningful corrective feedback, we can get 70% of our students to achieve what only 20% of them could without this feedback. By incorporating the type of instructional methods present in tutorial instruction, we can have 90% of all students performing at the level that only 20% of them can with classroom instruction. Bloom sought to determine which other alterable variables had such large effects on student performance; the results are shown in Table 3.1. Effect size is the number of standard deviations that student performance was affected by for each variable listed. It's evident from these data how dramatic an effect tutorial instruction has on student performance.

Can Mastery Learning Classrooms Be as Effective as Tutorial Instruction?

In the next two chapters of this book I will describe how mastery learning can be implemented in a classroom to individualize instruction, use formative assessment, and provide immediate, corrective feedback to come close to a tutorial instruction situation within a classroom. It will never replace the one-to-one instructional setting, but it comes far closer than a conventional classroom can. By having various learning opportunities and activities that students can choose from and the teacher can suggest for a particular student; having an immediate cycle of corrective feedback; allowing students to progress at their own pace; ensuring that students master content required by national, state, and district standards; and continuing to take advantage of small-group learning situations, a mastery learning classroom can come far closer to an individual tutoring experience than a conventional classroom.

Practical Implications of Mastery Learning

The research supports the belief that mastery learning results in improved student learning and motivation. But how do you actually *do* it? What are the implications of revamping a course to make it a mastery learning course? How do you handle the details of running the course in this way? In this chapter I will discuss the practical side of a mastery class.

"It's Not Fair"—or Is It?

I had to let go of many ideas about how to run a classroom to make the transition to a mastery learning environment. The first idea was my concept of "fair." I had the same concept of "fair" as my young children at home—everybody has to do the same thing for it to be "fair." I couldn't imagine how I could require one student to do more work than another without granting "extra credit." How could a classroom of teenagers operate when they knew that the kid next to them had to do more or fewer practice problems than they did? I was sure that there would be uproars of protest over it not being "fair."

But then I looked at it in a different way. Student A knows how to balance equations, remembers how to do this from physical science class, and can demonstrate that understanding to me very quickly. Is it "fair" to ask her to balance 30 of them when she doesn't need the extra practice just because another student does? Student B has practiced 30 of them and is still struggling. Is it "fair" to move on without him and say I've given him enough of a chance to learn because the average student in the room has gotten it? I came to see that a "fair" classroom is not one in which every student does the same number of practice problems, but one in which every student is given whatever support they need to achieve the same standard.

For a more in-depth discussion on this topic, read *Fair Isn't Always Equal* (Wormeli 2006).

Working With Students, Parents, and Administrators

As for my fear of the great uprising of students complaining that "it's not fair" for one to be sent back to do more practice problems while another is allowed to move on, it never happened. I taught over 200 students in this manner during the two years before writing this book—and not one of them ever made that complaint to me. I think it's all in the way that I introduced master learning and how I continued to talk about it throughout the year.

Introducing the concept of mastery learning

Many students fear that science (especially if it has a large amount of mathematical application) is too hard, abstract, and distant from their lives. They walk into the classroom with preconceptions and speculation about how they will not understand the content. Not all my students felt this way—but probably 70–75% of them were not at all sure that they could handle this course successfully and were just hoping to "get by." So after introducing myself on the first day of school, I told them that I believed that they all could learn it, I explained my dissatisfaction with the ability of students to skate by and pass without really ever learning anything, and I assured them that I would not move on without them nor would I hold anyone back who was ready to go on. I explained that I have enough respect for the students who get a concept to let them move on, and I have enough respect for the students who don't get a concept to stick with them until they get it. I truly believe that this approach was key to my successes with this teaching method—students saw me asking them to continue to work to understand a concept not as punishment, or busy work, but as a sign of respect that I believed they could "get it" and that I wouldn't move on without them until they did.

We talked about how it's not always the same students who "get" concepts quickly—one may be very good at mathematical problems and be able to zip through those concepts in the course, while another may be very good at spatial manipulations and be able to draw molecular structures with ease. Often, science and math courses build on prior knowledge. If students fail to understand the concepts that are introduced early in the year, they are doomed to a year of not understanding. However, if you take the time with students to make sure they really understand these earlier concepts, they are likely to be able to go much faster later on because they have a good foundation. I saw this to be true in my classroom after changing to mastery learning, and it was encouraging to the students.

We didn't get into too many details of how exactly the class would run on that first day; instead, I took them through the first few sections of the course to introduce them to the different choices and requirements they would have (see "Starting the Year" later in this chapter).

I introduced parents to the purpose behind and practical implications of mastery learning with the class syllabus (sent home the first day and posted on the class website), which included many of the same things I'd explained to the students on the first day of school. I also spent most of "Back to School Night" discussing how the class was going to run and why I was doing it this way. I found parents to be just as supportive as students—they really responded to the idea that their kids were going to get whatever they needed to learn and that it was going to be a flexible environment.

Handling lack of support

You may encounter people who are not supportive of your efforts to create a mastery learning environment. The students may be confused, early on, as to what to do. They're used to being told what to do each day and to being guided through a course as a group. But they're quick to catch on and soon they'll start voicing their desire for more classrooms to be run this way. Having a good picture ahead of time about how things are going to run and making sure that you have the infrastructure to support students will go a long way to cutting down on this period of "How does this work?" with the students.

Parents may question the change at first, but most will realize it's good for their students when you explain how things are running and why. It's hard for any parent to argue with a teacher who truly believes that all students can learn the material and will continue to work with the students in an individual way until they all accomplish the standards.

You're more likely to see lack of support from fellow teachers or administrators. People coming into your classroom won't see a neat, orderly classroom. Students will not all be doing the same thing. Some may be working individually, some in small groups, and some with you. There will be times when a student is waiting for something—for example, waiting to have a quiz graded by you in a one-on-one feedback session, or waiting for another student to be ready to do a lab so they can work together. But the "down time" in my mastery classroom was far, far less than the amount of time a student might *appear* to be listening to a lecture in my more traditional classroom and yet be completely unengaged.

4   Practical Implications of Mastery Learning

This is not to say that your room should be chaotic or that kids should be allowed to waste large amounts of time. You will have to move your eyes, and yourself, around the room and redirect students to get to work on the next task throughout the class period. But especially if you have block class periods, there likely will be a few minutes here and there where students are waiting for something or transitioning from one activity to another. And frankly, that's good for their brains! Everyone needs a few minutes here and there to transition or to relax. It's also not the worst thing in the world for my students to learn to have a little patience—to see that I'm working with another student and not yell my name across the room while I'm clearly busy simply because they need something right then and don't have the manners to wait. As the year progressed, my students showed great improvement in patience and politeness when working in a group setting!

Despite the benefits described above, when an administrator or a fellow teacher comes into your room, they may fear that you do not have things under control and that your students are not learning. Your best way to combat this is evidence. Keep track of evidence that shows how the students are learning. For example, I required every student to get an 80% on each section before moving on. Although I had no minimum grade requirements for chapter exams, because of the 80% requirement for mastery of each section it was very rare that anyone performed below a C level on a chapter exam. The chapter exams were no different than they'd been in previous years, yet there was a clear lack of D and F grades that had been present in previous years; this was a valid comparison to help convince administrators that the outcomes of this class were well worth the appearance of a "messy" classroom.

You may also meet resistance when students begin to talk with their friends. Word will spread about how different your classroom is, and soon other students may be asking their teachers, "Why can't our class be run like Mrs. So-and-So's?" Or as students pass out of your class and move on the next year, they may compare the classrooms and complain that they wish they were back in yours. It's hard for any teacher to hear that students wish that he or she were more like someone else. This may cause you to have resistance from your fellow teachers. Again, your best bet is to have some anecdotes and evidence ready when someone asks you about what you're doing. Never try to push a teaching method on someone else, but be open to sharing if someone shows interest.

In an ideal world you would have fully supportive administration and peers and you wouldn't have to deal with the problems I've described, but most teachers are not so lucky. If you encounter administrative resistance, you may not be able to go full-out to a full mastery learning classroom; instead, you may have to scale back and just implement some aspects of this type of classroom.

What Content Needs to Be Mastered?

When you require students to master content you need to think carefully about which content to require they master. As teachers, we tend to get caught up in the idea that everything we do is important and students should learn it all. But when implementing mastery learning you should consider what the key, essential concepts are that need to be mastered. For help in determining concepts that will appear on the mastery quizzes, look to the National Science Education Standards (NRC 1996), your state standards, and your school or district curriculum requirements. You will also want to require mastery of content that is a prerequisite for future content, to ensure that students are prepared for the future concepts.

It helps to keep the mastery quizzes brief—the more different concepts that are on the same quiz, the greater the likelihood that students won't pass it when they don't understand one of the concepts being tested. Break content down into single or two closely related concepts and have students "quiz out" of each concept as they go. This allows you to pinpoint and address specific misconceptions with students when you grade a quiz rather than having many areas of misunderstanding to work on. Shorter quizzes also allow you to grade them with the students as they finish taking them—a key component of effective, immediate feedback in a mastery course.

What Do You Consider "Mastery"?

You set the level of mastery in your course—is it 100%, 90%, 80%, 70%? I chose 80%. My quizzes generally had five questions on them, so a student who got four correct (80%) or 5 correct (100%) passed the quiz and could move on.

Keep in mind that students are sometimes exposed to a concept several times in a course. For example, students in my chemistry course were exposed to dimensional analysis on at least five separate occasions throughout the year in increasingly complex problems. I knew they would increase their ability to use the technique over the course of the year, so the initial quiz used fairly simple questions to get at the main concept of dimensional analysis. I knew that I would have later opportunities to assess their use of the technique in more complex situations, so I allowed the students to work up to those more difficult applications in quizzes as the year progressed. Although the requirement for mastery remained at 80% throughout the course as I assessed students using dimensional analysis in various settings, the level of difficulty of the problems increased and therefore my mastery requirements increased throughout the year for the use of that concept.

Grading

What to grade

Grade the work that will show you if the student has learned all that you want him or her to learn. For my upper-class courses, I graded three things: section quizzes, labs, and chapter tests. I did not grade worksheets, book questions, or anything else that I called a learning opportunity (see the section on learning opportunities later in this chapter). The point of a learning opportunity is to learn the skills that they then demonstrate on a lab or quiz. In the beginning, students will simply say, "If it's not graded then I won't do it." But they quickly learn that if they don't take advantage of some of the learning opportunities they most likely won't pass the quiz and will have to go back to learning again anyway. Within a week or two, most students have figured out that jumping the gun to the quiz just to get through it isn't the most efficient path through the course.

What you grade may depend on the level of the student as well. My junior- and senior-level courses were not required to complete any of the learning opportunities, but my younger students were required to complete a minimum of three learning opportunities before attempting the quiz. This requirement with younger students provided needed structure, but they still had flexibility because they could choose which three learning opportunities they wanted to complete. With my freshmen students, I graded their minimum required number of learning opportunities, but did so on completion credit (they received credit for work completed rather than accuracy of that work). They soon learned that even though the learning opportunities were graded on completion credit, not doing them correctly would lead to failed quizzes and having to start over again.

Students who don't finish

A very common question from my peers was "But what about a student who doesn't finish the curriculum?" We as teachers are so concerned with "getting through the curriculum" to prepare students for the next course that we often forget that "getting through" and "learning" can be two very different things. I had to remind myself, and others, on several occasions that I'd rather see students *learn* eight chapters of the course than see them just "get through" all nine chapters. As for students being prepared for the next course, the same applies—I would much rather have a student coming into my room who mastered most of the previous course than one who simply "went through" all of it. Usually, whenever I put it this way, others would agree.

But even so, you will need to have a plan for those who don't finish. Include in your syllabus how the grading will be adjusted for those who don't finish all the required sections or standards for your course. Each situation may be different. For my classroom, we did approximately four to five chapters per semester. I decided to deduct one letter grade for each chapter not completed during the semester (prorating for partial chapters).

Whatever system you decide to use, step back and make sure it seems appropriate. For example, if a student completed one out of the four chapters in a semester, the highest grade he or she could earn would be a D. If the student only completed two out of the four chapters, the highest grade he or she could earn would be a C. I felt that those were appropriate standards based on the overall requirements for the semester to earn an A. Make sure that you're comfortable with whatever a student walking out of your classroom would earn; I was comfortable with a student earning no higher than a C for completing half the required work *at the mastery level*.

You'll need to be prepared for the possibility of students not completing work, but out of all my students, only 15% or so did not complete all the required chapters—and none of them were behind more than one chapter at the end of the year.

How Do You Report "Mastery"?

Although the previous section gave tips on grading students in a mastery classroom on the traditional letter-grading scale, there are other methods for reporting mastery. Most teachers will not have the luxury of deviating from the report card format used by the school and district they work in, but there may be ways to supplement the mandated reporting procedures.

Letter grades (or other "category"-based grading systems such as percentages, satisfactory/exemplary, etc.) are arbitrary. Each teacher has autonomy in determining how grading will be done. Compared with others who have taught the same class, I've sometimes been a harder "grader" than my colleagues and other times been an "easier" grader. Grading is subjective, has very little concrete meaning, and can vary widely among schools, districts, and even teachers within the same department teaching the same course. One school I taught in wished to set higher standards for their students and therefore changed the traditional 90% = A to 92% = A. The problem with this is that teachers just shifted their baselines after a while. An A student in a teacher's mind is still going to be an A student. So teachers, consciously or unconsciously, shifted their grading practices so that the student who would have received an A on the 90% cutoff scale was still getting an A on the 92% cutoff scale. Changing the scale didn't really change the expectations in most classrooms in that school.

Standards-based grading and reporting, however, aren't as easy to shift as the more arbitrary grading systems commonly in practice. A standards-based grading system would begin with agreement by teachers, administrators, and curriculum advisers in the school or district as to the essential skills and standards in the course. These skills and standards may be based on national, state, district, or course standards, but those can sometimes be rather vague and may need to be further defined for reporting purposes. Once the essential content and skills for the course have been determined, a reporting system (either officially supported by the district or as a supplement you send to parents or include at parent-teacher conferences) can be developed to indicate each student's progress toward very objective standards or goals for the course.

Standards-based grading and reporting is a major topic on its own and cannot be done justice in this book; for more information on this topic read *Developing Standards-Based Report Cards* (Guskey and Bailey 2010).

Providing Meaningful Feedback

Answer keys

Practice does not make perfect—practice makes *permanent*. **Perfect practice makes perfect.** We've all had students who complete a long assignment practicing a particular type of problem—but they make the same mistake each time. It is extremely hard to break them of that mistake. This is why I encouraged my students to come check their work after a problem or two—and as they gained increasing confidence, they were encouraged to check their work after several practice problems. I had one major ground rule for the answer keys: They remain at the front of the room in the designated area (to prevent students from constantly asking, "Where's the answer key book?").

I used several three-ring binders and put answers in sequentially, with one binder for "book questions," one for "worksheets," and so on. I found that by splitting up the different types of answer keys students were less likely to have to wait for someone to finish looking at the keys. Use of the binders was important to make sure things didn't get scattered all over and misplaced.

With practice problems my work was shown so the students could try to find their mistake. If they couldn't find their mistake they were encouraged to come consult with me to get them back on track. Students would often send a representative of their small group to the front of the room to check their work. Sometimes they'd check after a single problem, and sometimes they would do several before checking—depending on the difficulty of the problems and their confidence in their ability to solve them.

I didn't grade the practice sheets or book questions, so it didn't matter to me if the students copied, because they weren't getting a grade for copied work. And they very quickly learned that copying the correct answers got them nowhere—they didn't get a grade for it *and* they didn't learn what they needed to learn to pass the quiz, so there was no benefit to them for that behavior. This was a crucial component, I believe, in the difference in actual learning that went on in my mastery classroom as opposed to "grade earning" in years past. The students and I could pinpoint mistakes in operation, understanding, application, or simple arithmetic very early in the practice process while their thought process was still fresh in their minds and could be altered.

Quizzes

Students would take a quiz and then come have it graded immediately (or after waiting a few minutes for me to finish with another student). They stood there with me while I graded the quiz, and I talked about what I was seeing and what mistakes I was correcting. The students' thought process on answering the questions was fresh in their minds, just as it was when they checked practice problems immediately with the answer key, and we could talk about any mistakes they made. These discussions would sometimes clear up misunderstandings, and I knew from simply talking to them that they were ready for another version of the quiz. Other times, I could tell they still weren't quite there yet, and depending on the nature of their confusion or misunderstanding I could suggest specific learning opportunities that would be most beneficial to where they were in the learning process at that moment—a truly individualized learning experience.

Labs

Unlike short quizzes, labs cannot be graded at the moment they are completed. I had students turn the labs into a tray to be graded when I had time. However, students "checked out" of lab by briefly explaining to me their understanding of the key points of the lab or their conclusions. This usually took no more than a minute or two for me to ask a few questions to ensure they'd gotten what I wanted them to get out of the lab experience. Sometimes, students were asked to think about something in a different way, look at their data again, or even repeat a trial if they had done something to provide invalid results.

Socially Constructed Understanding

Cooperative learning

Another question frequently asked by my peers interested in this teaching approach was, "But what about the richness of discussions and socially constructed understanding?" And my answer was, "It still occurs every day." My students were not working in isolation. They often worked with two or three other students. As I moved in and out of these small groups throughout a class period, I would sometimes catch what someone was saying and lead an impromptu discussion on everything from metacognition or study skills to the application of the concept they were learning about in some aspect of their lives. Students still benefited from the opportunity to try to explain something to another student, to have a fellow student explain something to them in a way that I hadn't thought of, and to build off other students' understanding to create a larger group-generated understanding.

These work groups were very dynamic; their composition changed regularly as a result of students being at different levels. Sometimes change came about because a group moved on while a student was absent; other times students started out working with friends but quickly learned that some people in the group passed quizzes before others in the group, thus making it necessary to find different groups ready for the same content. It did not take long for students to move out of the comfort zone of working with friends and instead work with other students at the same level.

Lectures and group discussions

Lectures still existed in this mastery classroom format—just in a far more useful and effective way. Usually a lecture would come about when a group of three to four students said they needed me to explain something to them, and I'd ask other students working on the same section if they wanted to join in. Then this small group of students (usually 3 to 10) would gather around the front demonstration table by the whiteboard while I gave a mini-lecture or held a small-group discussion. I would explain concepts, demonstrate a problem-solving technique, or discuss common misconceptions just as I would in a whole-class lecture/discussion in previous years. The difference was that in these mini-lectures, every one of the student participants was ready for that information at that moment. They were more engaged, there were no behavior management issues, and the lectures were far more effective at including student input. Yes, I would have to repeat the same "lecture/discussion" several times in a given class at various times in the week or month. But how many times did I have to repeat the same information to students who hadn't been listening or ready for the content during the whole-class version in previous years? It worked out to be about the same—but repeating the information to a "fresh audience" that was ready for the information was far more tolerable to me than repeating it to students who were not ready for it or did not pay attention.

These mini-lectures still resulted in those wonderful moments of interesting, thought-provoking, and "lightbulb" moment side discussions as had occurred in previous years of whole-class lectures/discussions; in fact, there were probably more of those moments because more students were engaged in these mini-lectures. These side discussions are valuable to the course and the student, but they are, by definition, spontaneous—you can't plan for them because you didn't know a student was going to "take it there."

In summary, my mastery classroom did not turn into a room full of individuals isolated from one another. Rather, it became a very dynamic, social, and spontaneous learning environment—one that embodied many of the reasons I went into teaching in the first place.

Taking Another Look at Your Curricular Materials

Before you read about learning opportunities, labs, and assessments in the next few pages, it's important that you take a fresh look at what materials and activities you use in your course. Earlier in this chapter, I discussed how important it is to really think about what needs to be mastered in your course. What are the specific goals and outcomes of the class and of each chapter or section? It's very important to think about those things when creating the mastery quizzes, as well as learning opportunities and activities, for your students.

It's very easy over the years to accumulate activities, worksheets, lessons, and other curricular items into the hodgepodge that is your course. I would keep labs the students and I liked, add in a "cool" way to practice a skill here, and tweak various aspects from year to year. But after a few years, I would sometimes step back and think to myself " When I put all of this together, is this really the most cohesive, efficient way to meet the course goals?" Sometimes the answer was "yes," but other times the answer was "no," so I'd make changes.

Mastery learning is a very goal/standards-driven type of classroom. Again, don't confuse this with "teaching to the test" (of which I'm definitely not a fan!). If I'm going to require students to master content before they're allowed to move on, then I had better really define what "master" is and what "content" they have to "master." I'm not "teaching to the test" for the sake of the test—I'm deciding what I think is important for them to learn and then creating tests to measure those things and curricular materials to prepare for those tests. In this way I'm testing to ensure they're getting what I want them to get. The test is a *tool* in this way of thinking, rather than the end goal.

Grant Wiggins and Jay McTighe have a method for doing just this—designing the assessment and the course materials with the end in mind—known as Understanding by Design. It's a backward-design process where teachers design assessment, course materials, and experiences based on what they want student to learn (the outcomes). You can read more about their process for designing a course with the end goals in mind at their website (UbD Exchange): *www.ubdexchange.org*.

Learning Opportunities

I no longer called anything an assignment; instead, I now used the term *learning opportunity*. I found this simple change in name could change the emphasis from "this was assigned so I have to do it but I don't really see why other than to get points" to "the reason I'm doing this is to learn." The exact list of learning opportunities available for each section varied depending on the nature of that section, but the following options were often included:

- Guided reading worksheets
- Answering questions at the end of the section in the book
- Practice worksheets for sections that included practicable skills
- Watching a narrated PowerPoint lecture on the classroom computers (more information about this is in the "Use of Technology" section later in this chapter)
- Taking notes
- Creating diagrams or drawings
- Filling in content organizers
- Discussing a concept with peers or with me

I would sometimes suggest or steer students toward a particular choice for a particular section depending on the concept involved, but the students were free to choose one or more of the learning opportunities based on their preferences. For example, some students clearly preferred to read the material with the help of the guided reading worksheet, while others preferred to watch the narrated PowerPoint and take notes.

All learning opportunities and lab worksheets were housed in a filing cabinet students could access. I didn't make enough copies of any learning activity for all students, because not every student will choose every learning opportunity. You'll begin to see which ones your students favor, or be able to anticipate that for a specific section most of them will choose the worksheet to practice a specific skill. You can always make more copies as necessary.

Labs

Labs may be one of the most challenging aspects of teaching a science course in the mastery classroom manner. My classroom had the lab in the back half of the room and the student seats in the front half. It was possible for my students to do a lab on any day they were ready. I set up bins (or tubs) for a particular lab with all the equipment needed. In the beginning, you'll need several bins as groups start off with labs at the same point. However, as they moved through the course, I found that having two bins for each lab was plenty for this type of setup.

Students would let me know they were ready for a lab, and I'd find partners for them (sometimes asking them to wait 5 to 10 minutes for someone else to be ready if there was no one ready at that moment). I'd grab a bin for that lab and take the students back to a lab table. I'd talk them through whatever information I would have said to the whole class before a lab. They could call me over at any time during the lab, and I often made visits back there to check on things. They "checked out" of lab as described earlier in this chapter.

Some teachers don't have the lab in the same room as their classroom. Although it's not as flexible as my setup described above, you can designate one or two days per week as "lab days," and anyone who is ready for a lab can do it at that time. If a student is not ready for a lab, he or she can continue with regular work for the class in the lab room.

Assessments

Quizzes are so commonplace in this type of classroom that they become very low-risk, and that helps keep nerves down. Students with test anxiety quickly overcome their fear of these quizzes because they know the quizzes are short, are done with little fanfare, and can be retaken until they pass.

To help create this atmosphere of low risk, treat quizzes as formative assessments. If a student passes a quiz, then you know he or she is ready to move on. When a student does not pass, talk with the student to figure out where he or she is making mistakes and which learning opportunities can help the student prepare to retake the quiz. This key component of mastery learning really moves students beyond the "What's my grade?" mentality and into the more reflective "What were my mistakes?" thought process.

Rapid repeaters

Some students will want to jump the gun to take a quiz just to get it over with, and then they'll want you to give them another one right after failing the first one just to get it over with. However, they will quickly learn that it will do them no good to continue to operate like this and that the only way they're going to pass the quiz is to be prepared for it. Throughout the year, students will become much better at recognizing when they understand something and are ready to demonstrate this understanding versus when they still need to keep working and practicing before taking the quiz. Some students will reach this self-regulation stage faster than others.

In the beginning of the year, allowing rapid retakes is fairly effective in teaching this lesson about recognizing when one is ready to take a quiz—the number of times that students have to attempt a quiz before passing it rapidly tapers off. However, you'll have some habitual rapid quiz takers who continue to take quizzes when they aren't ready and don't seem to learn this lesson. You can require these students to complete another learning activity before attempting the quiz after a failed attempt.

Logistics

You'll need more versions of the quizzes in the beginning of the year than later on. Most students will stop needing so many tries after a few sections. Retake numbers may jump up briefly during a difficult section, but, in general, most students get the hang of knowing when they're ready for a quiz. You can have 5 to 10 versions of a quiz collated and stored in a file box or cabinet. When a student is ready for a quiz, grab the first one in the folder. The chances are slim that if they come up for a retake they'll end up with the same version again.

If you have access to colored paper, you can copy quizzes on this paper to allow you to quickly scan the room and know which students have quizzes on their desk. You may also designate a space in your classroom as a quiz-taking area to allow you to keep an eye on students.

If a student fails a quiz, return the failed quiz so that he or she can continue to review the mistakes that you have discussed. However, students must give you the failed quiz in order to get another version. This handing in of failed quizzes keeps students from accumulating all the versions and sharing them with each other.

The first year I had a mastery learning classroom, I let students keep their passed quizzes so they could use them to study and review for the chapter exam. However, all the different versions I'd created soon accumulated among the students. After I noticed this, I developed a system for storing passed quizzes for students. Each student had a file folder in my file cabinet and I placed passed quizzes in the folder. When a student was reviewing for the chapter exam, they were allowed to have their folder to look over past quizzes. They handed the folder back in when leaving the room or asking for their chapter test.

Managing and Monitoring Progress

I used various tools to manage and monitor progress, including chapter checklists for students, a grid of quiz scores, and a classroom calendar.

Student checklists

Students were given a chapter checklist (see example in appendix) at the start of each chapter. The front page of the checklist packet had space for the students to record what their goals were for that day. When students came into the classroom, this checklist helped them remember what they did the day before and focus on their goals for that day. (This served as the "bell work" for each class that was required in my school.)

Inside the checklist packet was information for each section in that chapter. It provided section goals to help students know if they were ready to take a quiz for that section. It also provided a list of possible learning opportunities for a section as well as required activities (such as a lab). A suggested completion date and a space for them to record their actual completion date were included in the checklist. This packet served as a guideline and a way for students to monitor their own progress, taking a level of responsibility for their own learning. Students turned in the checklist with the chapter test.

Quiz score records

Although it's certainly possible to record the number of attempts each student completes for each section, I simply recorded the score for each passed quiz. I kept a grid with student names down the left and section numbers across the top (see example in appendix). When a student passed a quiz, I'd write in the score for that section. I had a visual assessment of where a class was and how fast they were moving. I'd then enter scores into the computerized gradebook when I had time.

Classroom calendar

I kept a calendar on the whiteboard at the front of the room that had a suggested course of action for the week. Students understood that if they were close to my suggestions they'd complete the work required for the maximum possible grade for the year. They also knew that it was within their control to speed up and catch up if they began to fall behind for any reason—including absences.

Incorporating Progress Into Student Grades

As mentioned earlier in the "Grading" section, if students in my mastery learning classroom failed to complete the course requirements, their grade was reduced. You can also include a daily "work" component in the grade. Making daily progress and work ethic worth 10% of the grade for the semester goes a long way toward motivating many students and toward giving consequences for those not working to their potential. It's not about how quickly they complete work; rather, it's about whether they are on task and engaged appropriately throughout the class period. Some students may complete work very quickly and be maintaining adequate progress toward the semester goals—but if they can do a section and take the quiz in half of a class period and then waste the other half because they'll still finish on time, that's not exactly the point.

Keeping Pace With Students

Your first year, you'll have students who move quickly, and you have to stay ahead of them. You'll have to make sure you have the learning opportunities, quizzes, and tests prepared and copied in time for them. You'll also need to make sure you have labs set up before they are ready for them. The second year will be much easier because a lot of the work will have already been done—only revised and new materials will need to be created.

Students who finish early

You will most likely have students who finish the content early. What then? I allowed my students to design a project or topic to study of interest to them. If they completed such projects I awarded extra credit. If they did not complete such projects, then their daily participation grade would suffer, since they were no longer working on either course requirements or enrichment opportunities. Usually, if they were learning about something they were interested in, and if they were given freedom in how that new knowledge was demonstrated, they were happy to work on the project. I received wonderful reports, presentations, posters, children's books, coloring books, pop-up books, game boards, videos, poetry, plays, and other examples of creative ways to show understanding of topics of interest to the students and to extend their understanding of course material.

Students who move too slowly

It's important to understand why a student isn't progressing as quickly as you'd like. Is it because of habitual absences? Is it because of lack of effort? Or is it because the material is difficult for them? Each of these reasons warrants a different course of action.

Habitual absences should be dealt with in your classroom as they are within your school. Lack of effort can be discussed with the student to determine the cause. Is there anything you can do to make the content more relevant for that particular student? Can you offer assistance in a rough spot for them to make it over a hump and then continue to progress?

If the material is simply more difficult for certain students and that is causing them to move more slowly than you'd like, know that at least they are being allowed to understand material as they go. I'd rather have students like this end up understanding most of what they were supposed to learn in the year rather than being exposed to it all but not understanding. Moving slowly with appropriate effort and work ethic in class is completely acceptable in my mind. I'd rather students have the success of succeeding at what they are attempting and not cover as much content than leave them behind early in the year knowing they can never catch up.

Accumulating Background Knowledge

Many of the students who move slowly in the beginning because of difficulty with the content will actually begin to catch up. I believe this happens for two important reasons. First, they see that you won't "give up on them" by moving on when the majority of the class is ready. They understand that you will continue to work with them at their level to help them be successful and understand the content. This increases self-confidence and self-efficacy, which often increases performance as well.

Second, as students understand the more basic, background, or foundational content in the beginning of the year, they begin to move more quickly through the application of that content later in the year. Instead of never understanding the later information because of a lack of foundation, they have a solid foundation and therefore the gap closes between them and students who find the content less challenging.

Use of Technology

There are many ways in which technology helped me run a mastery classroom, and I'm sure there are many more ways other teachers will use new and creative technology to offer mastery courses.

Narrated presentations and podcasting

Each section in my course had a PowerPoint presentation. I used the "narrate" feature in PowerPoint to add voice-overs to the presentations as if I was giving a lecture. These narrated files are large in size, so they need to be changed to other formats with smaller file sizes to be published online for student access. There are many programs to convert PowerPoint files to movie files or web pages; one example is Impatica (*www.impatica.com*). Many of these companies offer educational pricing to teachers, so always check with their customer service departments before purchasing. There are also free programs and services, such as authorPoint Lite and authorStream, which allow you to upload narrated presentations and store them online for students to access (visit *www. authorgen.com* for more information).

Narrated presentations can also be converted to MP4 format (or podcast) for viewing on mobile devices with programs like those available at *www.ppt-to-dvd.com*. Podcasts (the MP4 files) can be uploaded and housed in iTunes (*www.itunes.com*) or on your classroom website. Search the internet for ways to convert PowerPoint to Flash, web page, MP4, or MPEG. There will undoubtedly continue to be new and different ways to convert presentations to smaller and more mobile formats, so find a way that works for you, your technology, and your budget.

Classroom websites

Having a classroom website, either through your school or district's website or through one of the free teacher website hosting services (e.g., *www.schoolrack.com*

or *www.educatorpages.com*) allows your students to access your information any-where. You can have a page describing mastery learning and the class structure in general and then a page for each chapter. Each chapter's page can contain the files for the chapter checklist, learning opportunities, narrated presentations, and other resources for that chapter. Students can use classroom computers, library computers, home computers, mobile devices, or laptops if you're a one-to-one school or have mobile classrooms available.

Course management sites

There are many course management systems available. They can house all docu-ments, administer online tests, keep track of grades, lock and unlock materials based on a student's progress, contain "drop boxes" for students to submit work to you, house discussion boards and collaborative documents, and much more. Some systems cost money and you may have access to them through your school district (e.g., Blackboard, WebCT, or WebTrain); other systems are free but may require you to have access to a web hosting system (e.g., Moodle). An online search for any of these specific systems or for "course management systems" will present you with information and options to fit your available technology, support, and needs.

Assessment creators

Many textbooks now come with EXAMVIEW software (*www.einstruction.com*). These computerized question banks can be invaluable in creating multiple ver-sions of assessments for mastery learning. Not only can EXAMVIEW choose questions at random given your specifications of what content and type of ques-tion to create multiple quizzes, it also has the ability to randomize variables within a question. Some question banks from textbook publishers already con-tain variables that can be randomized (such as the mass and volume in a density question), but if you don't have access to already created questions, you can create your own questions with randomized variables within the software. You may even have the infrastructure to allow these multiple versions to be posted online or on a building's intranet and allow students to use classroom comput-ers or laptops to take quizzes online.

Online testing

Often, the exam software provided by the publisher of your textbook, or even an online portal provided by the publisher, will allow you to administer online testing. Some of these systems require additional fees and others do not, so be sure to investigate the options available with your specific adopted curriculum. Course management systems also offer the availability of online testing. Some systems are stand-alone testing systems, such as ClassMarker (*www.classmarker.*

com), which is available for about $25 per year for teachers. An internet search of "online testing" will provide you with current options.

Some online tests are static—the questions you choose are the only ones the student will see. This doesn't work so well for repeated mastery testing, because the student will figure out the correct answers to those specific questions and pass the quiz without really mastering the content. Systems such as ClassMarker allow for randomized questions—you tell it what kind and how many and it will provide each student with a randomized test.

Immediate, individualized feedback is one of the key aspects of mastery learning. With this in mind, set up your online testing routines to include that important type of feedback. The benefit of online testing is that you often do not have to grade the tests yourself—the computer will do it. However, the drawback is that this takes away the moment of you grading the quiz with your student and providing that immediate, individualized feedback. I encourage you to develop a routine that includes personal, one-on-one feedback, reviewing each computerized test with any student who did not pass.

The limitations of the available formats for online testing constitute a second possible drawback. These systems are not always capable of having students show work or write in specific formats; for example, entering equations, complicated expressions, or anything with subscripts and superscripts (such as chemical formulas) is not often possible. You may teach a course in which that isn't a problem for you, but in some cases it may hinder your ability to use online testing.

Starting the Year

A mastery class is very different from other classes students have experienced. I found it was better to ease them into it rather than to just say "go." On the first day of class I talked about what a mastery class is and how it was going to work. I continued to emphasize the key points throughout the first week or two—that self-paced wasn't self-taught, that every student was responsible for learning, that no student would move on until he or she had learned the material, and that I wouldn't give up on a student until he or she had learned the material.

For the first few sections of the curriculum, I led them through the process. We got out the chapter checklist first thing in each class period and walked through how to fill out the first page with our goals for the day. Then we looked at the information in the chapter checklist and talked through the different options to learn the material in the first section. For each of the first three sections, I chose a different learning opportunity to lead the class through, to show them the various options they had available when they were free to choose their own learning opportunities. During these sections, I introduced the various systems of the course—where to get worksheets, how to look at the section's goals to determine if they were ready for the quiz, how to ask for a quiz, how to take a quiz, how to have a quiz graded, how to complete a lab, and so on. After the third section of the chapter, they were free to begin choosing how they learned and working at their own pace.

It's important to model the self-directed learning process for them in the beginning. The younger your students, the more sections or days you'll need to continue modeling this process. But you need to remember to not hold students back who are ready to move on while you're getting other students up to speed on the logistics of the course.

Summary

In this chapter I've discussed a number of the practical aspects of mastery learning—from how to determine what your students will be "mastering" to how to develop and deliver learning opportunities and mastery assessments in the classroom and through the use of technology. In the next chapter, I'll describe what my mastery learning classroom looked like and present several variations that could be used to make mastery learning fit specific circumstances or people.

How Mastery Learning Might Look

The Full Mastery Learning Classroom

Although this section describes my chemistry classroom, the procedures can be modified to fit any grade level or content area.

Each day, students entered the room, pulled out their chapter checklist (see appendix) to remember where they left off the day before, and set their goals for that day. They would consult the classroom calendar on the whiteboard where I'd posted my "suggested" sections to complete each day. Students could use this information to determine if they were approximately on track or if they were falling behind and needed to catch up. They would also consult the possible learning opportunities and any required activities for that section in their chapter checklist.

After setting their goals for that day, they'd begin working. If they needed a worksheet, reading guide, or lab sheet, they'd go to the student-accessible filing cabinet and pull out whatever sheets they needed. If they were choosing to view a narrated presentation, they would move to a classroom computer. Students needing to work on a lab would find a partner or ask me if anyone else needed to do that lab, and then they'd let me know they were ready for lab bins and instructions. Students would move from one activity to another throughout the 90-minute block period.

I was always busy—floating between lab groups to check on progress and safety, stopping by a student standing at the answer key in the front of the room who was puzzled about why he didn't get the correct answer on a practice sheet, holding a mini-lecture with a few students at the front of the classroom, and handing out and grading quizzes. Students may have had to wait a few minutes for my attention, but they quickly learned that the one-on-one attention would come. They also learned nonscience skills such as waiting for me to come to them rather than yelling my name across the room or coming up and starting to talk to me even though I was clearly working with another student at that time.

I used my teacher grading sheet to do a quick visual check at the beginning and end of each class period and, if necessary, reminded students to move a little more quickly or assess why they were falling behind.

In the beginning, things didn't move so smoothly. At first, students tended to ask for quizzes before they were ready for them. They looked for the learning opportunity that was "easiest to complete." They were not very good at assessing if they understood material and were ready to take a quiz or move on. However, by the end of the first semester they were much better at judging their own understanding and at selecting learning opportunities that would provide better understanding for different types of information (for example, students soon discovered that working on a practice worksheet when a math skill was involved was an effective use of time). By the end of the second semester, students were quite good at these things and actually very rarely needed to retake a quiz.

To an outside observer, my classroom looked more "messy" than before. Students worked individually or in small groups, in various parts of the room doing all sorts of different activities. They were performing lab investigations, practicing with worksheets, finding a quiet corner of the room to read while completing a reading guide, learning from a presentation on a computer, taking quizzes, or standing around up front with me and a few other students participating in a small-group discussion. From time to time, a student might take a "mental break" for a few minutes and chat with friends or look up the scores from a big game on a classroom computer. But as I floated around the room, I'd make sure those mental breaks didn't last too long. Overall, during each 90-minute period, each student was actively engaged for a far greater period of time, even with periodic mental breaks, than when I ran my classroom in a more traditional manner. Besides, even I need to take mental breaks in a 90-minute period!

Overall, I had a much greater handle, even with the "messy" environment, on where each student stood, what they were working on, how they preferred to operate, and their strengths and weaknesses far earlier in the school year than ever before. I spent more individual time with each student than in my previous years of teaching and got to know them, both academically and personally, much more quickly.

Variation 1: Weekly Group Discussions

During the second year of mastery teaching, I had some students who, although they loved this setup, wanted a small period of time for a more formal group discussion. Out of my four sections of chemistry, students in two of the sections wanted this opportunity. To meet this request by students, I started doing a more formal discussion session in the last class period of the week. Before the discussion section I would determine what most of the students in the class were working on or getting ready to work on, and then I would create a short presentation to guide the discussion using clickers (remote devices allowing students to respond to questions or polls within the presentation) to highlight the main concepts they either just finished or were about to start. I didn't go into details of how to solve a particular type of math problem in the class, but rather kept it more "big picture" to give kids an overall direction and feeling of how things fit together. The clickers kept students motivated and provided me with feedback on how they were understanding concepts.

Not all students chose to participate in the presentation/group discussion. I allowed students who were either ahead of or behind others in the class, or who just had other work for the course they wanted or needed to accomplish, to opt out of the discussion. The only rule was that they had to be quiet during that time so as not to disturb the presentation/discussion.

The addition of this presentation/discussion component to my class is an example of how flexible the mastery learning format is. A group of students expressed a desire to have a large-group "big picture" discussion once a week, and I incorporated it into the course. Other students didn't want to have that experience, so they continued to do other class work. Mastery learning is completely customizable to you and your students.

Variation 2: Requiring Learning Opportunities

For younger students (see example in the next paragraph) or for teachers who may not be ready or able to fully implement mastery learning, you can incorporate some aspects without completely revamping your classroom.

The freshmen in my physical science course, like the older students, were given the chapter checklists and were not allowed to move on to another section until passing the quiz. However, the younger students had more frequent presentations/group discussions that were not optional, and they were required to complete three learning opportunities before attempting the quiz. Although even the older students would have a tendency to attempt quizzes before they were ready in the beginning of the year, they learned fairly quickly that it's counterproductive to do this. The younger students, on the other hand, tended not to learn this lesson quite so quickly. Depending on the group of students, I would release this requirement near the end of the year and allow them to choose how-ever many learning opportunities they needed to complete in order to learn. I would sometimes open this restriction in the last chapter or the last quarter of the year, depending on the progress of the students toward self-regulation.

Variation 3: Group Labs

You may wish to hold labs all at the same time—for logistical reasons, safety reasons, or your own personal comfort with the variety of activities happening in your room at the same time. Students may have a designated day during the week for completing labs, and during that designated day they can complete any lab they are ready for. With full mastery learning, individual students com-plete a lab when they are ready for it and therefore will be completing labs at various times. However, labs can also be completed together as an entire class, as they would in a more traditional classroom. Please be careful about separat-ing labs from the other course work students do in the classroom. Labs are most effective at increasing understanding when they are completed in conjunction with other learning opportunities for that same content.

Variation 4: Mastery Outside of Class Time

I know some colleagues who still require mastery of content but, rather than allowing all students to work at their own pace or holding all students up until all have mastered the content, require the repetition of quizzes and additional learning opportunities to take place outside of class time. This might occur dur-ing a seminar or study hall period, or before or after school. This fits into a more traditional classroom structure, but be aware that if students are not mastering content before you move on in the classroom, they will continue to fall behind. Likewise, they may feel punished by having to come in after school or at other times to pass. Allowing all students to progress at their own pace, if it's possible in your situation, ensures that no one falls further and further behind and that all students are shown the respect of being allowed to move at their own pace.

Variation 5: Layered Curriculum

Layered Curriculum (*www.help4teachers.com*) is another course format to allow students to take control of their own learning by allowing them to choose how they learn, how they demonstrate that knowledge, and what grade they choose to earn. With Layered Curriculum, students are given a menu from which to choose their learning activities. The menu is broken down into "C-level," "B-level," and "A-level" sections. Each level contains a list of learning opportunities and the number of points each activity is worth. Students begin on the C-level menu and choose activities to reach a certain point maximum (designated by you). Once they have achieved the C-level maximum, they may move onto the B level and choose learning opportunities until they reach the maximum number of points at that level. Finally, students move on to the A-level section of the menu.

Layered Curriculum works well with mastery learning. Using Layered Curriculum with mastery learning may allow a teacher to transition from a traditional classroom without making drastic changes. Teachers may keep students together by giving all students a deadline to complete a menu. This way, all students will be working on the same content, and they can take exams and do other activities together as they work to meet the deadline. In full mastery learning, there are no such deadlines other than the end of the course.

Mastery learning deducts points at the end for those who did not complete all the components. In Layered Curriculum, the teacher can still move the class on from one menu to another, and the level of the menu reached will determine the grade. In Layered Curriculum, not every student will have mastered every piece of the content before the class moves on, but each student will receive the grade for the level he or she completed on the menu. Perhaps a slower student will only complete the C level of the menu and therefore will receive a maximum of a C grade. In mastery learning, a student may have completely mastered all of the content he or she was exposed to during the course but may not complete all the chapters and therefore would end up with a lower grade. It's the difference between covering all the content with every student having various levels of mastery of each part of the curriculum versus all students mastering content with different amounts of content covered.

Summary

I t's very daunting to consider completely changing the way your classroom is run. I went back and forth many times in the month before school started before I made the switch to mastery learning. I knew my students would benefit, but it is a lot of work to set up the learning opportunities and quizzes in the first year. I also knew there would be challenges with convincing students, parents, colleagues, and administrators that this was a step in the right direction for my classroom. It was a bumpy road at first—figuring out all the different ways kids would try to cheat the system and finding the "bottlenecks" in the system.

The results were well worth any bumps. Kids took responsibility for their own learning, they enjoyed the freedom to choose how they progressed through content, and the format provided wonderful flexibility for students missing class for illness, appointments, or sports. The best result was that students felt respected in the classroom: Those who could move more quickly and didn't need to complete as much practice to gain a new skill appreciated the fact that I respected their ability to move on when they were ready; those who needed more time and would have been left behind had I moved the class along together appreciated the respect I showed them in staying with each of them until they were ready to move on. This respect for both the upper and lower students resulted in higher motivation, better work ethic, and a greater appreciation for the material they were learning.

The switch doesn't need to be as dramatic as mine. I went from a traditional classroom to complete mastery learning all at once. However, you may not be ready for such a dramatic change. Try changing one chapter in your curriculum, or try a less open format for the course. As shown in Chapter 5, there are variations in how mastery learning can look in different classrooms at various levels of student autonomy. The results you see will convince you to continue moving in this direction.

Observations From My Mastery Learning Classroom

- There was a dramatic increase in student responsibility for learning.
- There was a large increase in student awareness of their own understanding of material and readiness to move on.
- There was an increase in how quickly I got to know each student, their strengths and weaknesses, academically and as individual people.
- The gap between students of different levels narrowed or closed—lower-level students started off more slowly but almost always caught up and sometimes even passed higher-level students.
- There was individual accountability—students could not ride the coattails of other classmates, and they figured this out rather quickly.
- There was flexibility—students chose which activities to learn from and could work ahead or catch up from absences or other issues.
- Students were not left behind when they didn't "get" content early on in the school year.
- There was increased engagement in learning—providing options and individual accountability increased student participation.
- My classroom was a little more "messy."
- I was busier during the actual class periods—helping students, grading quizzes, giving mini-lectures, supervising labs.
- Students felt respected and gained confidence that they could learn the material.
- The second year was much easier than the first!
- I was comfortable with each and every student walking out of my class with a passing grade as my "stamp of approval," knowing they'd learned the material and not just "gotten through" it.

The Second Year and Beyond

As every teacher knows, we're never done changing things. No lesson is perfect and nothing works for every class every year. What works wonderfully with one group of students may be a horrible disaster with another group. That's the art of teaching. And just like everything else, the first year of running a classroom this way will result in things you want to change for the next time. You'll figure out a better system for disseminating worksheets, determine a better method for monitoring quiz taking, develop new learning activities, and determine different points in the course where you may want to bring all the students back together.

Where to Find More Information

There are teachers out there who can share how they implement mastery learning, and it's very helpful to have people to whom you can direct questions when changing the structure of your classroom. For these reasons, I've created *www.ScienceMasteryLearning.com*, a place where teachers can share, discuss, and support mastery learning in science classrooms at all levels. As teachers share resources on mastery learning that they have found useful, we'll begin to build a resource clearinghouse.

References

Block, J. 1971. *Mastery learning: Theory and practice.* New York: Holt, Rinehart and Winston.

Bloom, B. S. 1968. Mastery learning. In *Evaluation comment.* Los Angeles: University of California at Los Angeles, Center for the Study of Evaluation of Instructional Programs.

Bloom, B. S. 1984. The 2 sigma problem: The search for methods of group instruction as effective as one-to-one tutoring. *Educational Researcher* 13 (6): 4–16.

Bruning, R. H., G. J. Schraw, M. M. Norby, and R. R. Ronning. 2004. *Cognitive psychology and instruction.* 4th ed. Upper Saddle River, NJ: Pearson Prentice Hall.

Clark, R., F. Nguyen, and J. Sweller. 2006. *Efficiency in learning: Evidence-based guidelines to manage cognitive load.* San Francisco: Pfeiffer.

Gallup, H. F. 1995. Personalized System of Instruction: Behavior modification in education. *http://ww2.lafayette.edu/~allanr/gallup.html*

Gallup, H. F., and R. W. Allan. 1996. Concerns with some recent criticisms of the Personalized System of Instruction (PSI). *http://ww2.lafayette.edu/~allanr/concerns.html*

Guskey, T., and J. Bailey. 2010. *Developing standards-based report cards.* Thousand Oaks, CA: Corwin.

Kalyuga, S., P. Ayres, P. Chandler, and J. Sweller. 2003. The expertise reversal effect. *Educational Psychologist* 38 (1): 23–31.

Keller, F. S. 1968. "Good-bye, teacher...." *Journal of Applied Behavioral Analysis* 1 (1): 79–89.

Kulik, C.-L. C., J. A. Kulik, and R. L. Bangert-Drowns. 1990. Effectiveness of mastery learning programs: A meta-analysis. *Review of Educational Research* 60 (2): 265–299.

McNeill, K., D. J. Lizotte, J. Krajcik, and R. W. Marx. 2006. Supporting students' construction of scientific explanations by fading scaffolds in instructional materials. *Journal of Learning Sciences* 15 (2): 153–191.

National Research Council (NRC). 1996. *National science education standards.* Washington, DC: National Academies Press.

Renkl, A., R. K. Atkinson, and U. H. Maier. 2000. From studying examples to solving problems: Fading worked-out solution steps helps learning. In *Proceedings of the 22nd annual conference of the Cognitive Science Society,* ed. L. Gleitman and A. K. Joshi, 393–398. Mahwah, NJ: Lawrence Erlbaum.

Sharpe, T. 2006. "'Unpacking" scaffolding: Identifying discourse and multimodal strategies that support learning. *Language and Education* 20 (3): 211–231.

Shell, D. F., D. W. Brooks, G. Trainin, K. M. Wilson, D. F. Kauffman, and L. M. Herr. 2010. The unified learning model: How motivational, cognitive, and neurobiological sciences inform best teaching practices. New York: Springer.

Van Merrienboar, J., L. Kester, and F. Paas. 2006. Teaching complex rather than simple tasks: Balancing intrinsic and germane load to enhance transfer of learning. *Applied Cognitive Psychology* 20 (3): 343–352.

Vygotsky, L. S. 1978. *Mind in society: The development of higher psychological processes,* ed. S. Cole, V. J. Scriber, and E. Souberman. Cambridge, MA: Harvard University Press.

Wood, D., J. Bruner, and G. Ross. 1976. The role of tutoring in problem solving. *Journal of Child Psychology and Psychiatry* 17 (2): 89–100.

Wormeli, R. 2006. *Fair isn't always equal: Assessing and grading in the differentiated classroom.* Portland, ME: Stenhouse Publishers.

Appendix

A

Example of Backwards-Faded Worksheet

Example of Student Chapter Checklist

Example of Teacher Grading Grid

EXAMPLE OF BACKWARDS-FADED WORKSHEET

Name _____ Date _____ Hr _____

Worksheet 1.4—Unit Conversions

1. Convert 20.33 cm to m

20.33 cm	0.01 m	
	1 cm	= 20.33 * 0.01 / 1 = 0.2033 m

2. Convert 12.06 L to cL

12.06 L	1 cL	
	0.01 L	= 12.06 * 1 / 0.01 = 1,206 cL

3. Convert 32.27 kg to g

32.27 kg	1,000 g	
	1 kg	= 32.27 * 1,000 / 1 =

4. Convert 13.09 m to cm

13.09 m	1 cm	
	0.01 m	=

5. Convert 3.47 mm to m

3.47 mm	m	
	mm	=

6. Convert 33.81 kg to g

33.81 kg		
	kg	=

7. Convert 9.92 kL to L

9.92 kL		
		=

Example of Backwards-Faded Worksheet *(continued)*

8. Convert 2.61 g to mg

$$\frac{2.61 \text{ g} \quad \bigg| \quad\quad\quad\quad\quad\quad}{\quad\quad\quad \bigg| \quad\quad\quad\quad\quad\quad} =$$

9. Convert 24.37 g to mg

10. Convert 28.77 L to cL

11. Convert 22.04 mL to L

12. Convert 9.42 L to mL

13. Convert 20.03 cm^3 to mL

14. Convert 23.28 L to mL

15. Convert 9.72 mL to L

16. Convert 1.47 kg to mg

$$\frac{1.47 \text{ kg} \quad \bigg| \quad\quad \text{g} \quad\quad \bigg| \quad\quad \text{mg}}{\quad\quad\quad \bigg| \quad\quad \text{kg} \quad\quad \bigg| \quad\quad \text{g}} =$$

17. Convert 7.18 mL to cL

$$\frac{7.18 \text{ mL} \quad \bigg| \quad\quad \text{L} \quad\quad \bigg| \quad\quad\quad}{\quad\quad\quad \bigg| \quad\quad\quad\quad \bigg| \quad\quad \text{L}} =$$

18. Convert 33.21 cg to mg

19. Convert 30.62 mg to cg

20. Convert 16.43 mg to cg

A Appendix

EXAMPLE OF STUDENT CHAPTER CHECKLIST

Chemistry Daily Journal   Unit #____3____

Today's Date	What did I accomplish yesterday?	What are my goals today? What sections, activities, labs do I want to get done today?

Example of Student Chapter Checklist *(continued)*

UNIT 3

Theme: Airbags

Essential questions:

1. How is science a human endeavor?

2. How do scientists work to gather, analyze, communicate, and validate data to form and change models?

3. How does matter undergo changes and how do we use chemical equations?

4. How do matter and energy interact?

Section	Objectives	Learning Opportunities (Check those that you complete)	Suggested Completion Date	Date Completed
3-1	• Distinguish between states of matter • Explain characteristics of different states of matter • Explain changes in states of matter	☐ Reading guide ☐ PowerPoint ☐ Practice 3-1 ☐ Discuss with peers ☐ Discuss with teacher		
3-2	• Distinguish between chemical and physical properties • Distinguish between extensive and intensive properties	☐ Reading Guide ☐ PowerPoint ☐ Practice 3-2 ☐ Discuss with peers ☐ Discuss with teacher		
3-3	• Define and calculate density • Lab 3.3: Use measurements of mass and volume with graphical analysis to determine density; define density as an intensive property	☐ **Lab 3.3—must complete first** ☐ Reading Guide ☐ PowerPoint ☐ Worksheet 3-3 ☐ Practice 3-3 ☐ Discuss with peers ☐ Discuss with teacher		
3-4	• Distinguish between chemical and physical changes • Lab 3.4: Observe chemical and physical changes	☐ **Lab 3.4—must complete first** ☐ Reading Guide ☐ PowerPoint ☐ Practice 3-4 ☐ Discuss with peers ☐ Discuss with teacher		

A | Appendix

Example of Student Chapter Checklist *(continued)*

Section	Objectives	Learning Opportunities (Check those that you complete)	Suggested Completion Date	Date Completed
3-5	• Define pressure and atmospheric pressure • Qualitatively relate properties of gases: volume, pressure, temperature, number of particles • Define kinetic molecular theory • Distinguish between real and ideal gases	☐ Reading Guide ☐ PowerPoint ☐ Practice 3-5 ☐ Discuss with peers ☐ Discuss with teacher		
3-6	• Define a mole and Avogadro's number • Define and calculate molecular mass • Define molecular mass and atomic mass as mass for one mole of particles • Perform calculations between number of particles, moles, and masses	☐ Reading Guide ☐ PowerPoint 3.6A ☐ Practice 3-6A ☐ PowerPoint 3.6B ☐ Practice 3-6B ☐ PowerPoint 3.6 C ☐ Practice 3-6 C ☐ Worksheet 3-6 ☐ Discuss with peers ☐ Discuss with teacher		
3-7	• Lab 3.7: Quantitatively relate gas properties of pressure, volume, and temperature • Introduce pressure units • Define and perform calculations with gas laws (Boyle's, Charles', Avogadro's, Combined, Ideal) • Define standard temperature and pressure	☐ Reading Guide ☐ PowerPoint 3-7 A ☐ Practice 3-7 A ☐ PowerPoint 3-7 B ☐ Practice 3-7 B ☐ Worksheet 3-7 ☐ **Lab 3-7—must complete after** ☐ Discuss with peers ☐ Discuss with teacher		

Example of Student Chapter Checklist *(continued)*

Section	Objectives	Learning Opportunities (Check those that you complete)	Suggested Completion Date	Date Completed
Final Chapter 3 Lab	• Observe chemical and physical process resulting in the production of a gas • Evaluate different processes for effectiveness based on criteria for a "good" airbag • Review writing chemical formulas and equations	☐ **Lab—must complete**		
Review & Test	• Demonstrate knowledge from Chapter 3	☐ Review section quizzes ☐ Chapter 3 review ☐ Discuss with peers ☐ Discuss with teacher		

EXAMPLE OF TEACHER GRADING GRID

Name	3-1	3-2	Lab 3-3	3-3	3-4	3-5	3-6	3-7	Lab 3-7	Test 3
Student A	4	5	22	4	5					
Student B	5	4	25	5	5	5	5	4	27	42
Student C	4	5	28	4	5	5				
Student D	5	5	25	5	4	5	4			
Student E	4	4	22	5						
Student F	5	4	25	4						

Teacher grading grids provide a quick visual check as to where various students are in their progress through the curriculum. This grid is an example for Chapter 3 (which has seven sections) for a class where each quiz is worth 5 points and students must score at least a 4 out of 5 to pass.

Labs are worth 30 points each. Some are meant to be completed before the section and others are to be completed after the section. You may wish to include labs in this grid to visually keep track of which students have completed which labs, or you may simply wish to keep them in the gradebook.

The test is worth 50 points.

Index